WORKBOOK

HARMONY

& VOICE LEADING

VOLUME I

FOURTH EDITION

EDWARD ALDWELL
The Curtis Institute of Music,
Mannes College of Music

CARL SCHACHTER
Mannes College of Music,
The Juilliard School

ALLEN CADWALLADER
Oberlin Conservatory of Music

KAREN BOTTGE
Editorial Consultant
University of Kentucky School of Music

SCHIRMER
CENGAGE Learning™

Australia • Brazil • Japan • Korea • Mexico • Singapore • Spain • United Kingdom • United States

For product information and technology assistance, contact us at
Cengage Learning Customer & Sales Support,
1-800-354-9706

For permission to use material from this text or product, submit all requests online at **www.cengage.com/permissions**
Further permissions questions can be e-mailed to
permissionrequest@cengage.com

ISBN-13: 978-1-4390-8325-3
ISBN-10: 1-4390-8325-8

Schirmer
20 Channel Center Street
Boston, MA 02210
USA

Cover image: © The Art Archive / Bach House Leipzig / Alfredo Dagli Orti

Cengage Learning products are represented in Canada by Nelson Education, Ltd.

For your course and learning solutions, visit
www.cengage.com

Purchase any of our products at your local college store or at our preferred online store
www.CengageBrain.com

Printed in the United States of America
2 3 4 5 6 7 14 13 12 11 10

CONTENTS

PREFACE

This workbook, together with the exercises in the text, should provide more than enough material for homework assignments, classroom demonstrations, and periodic reviews. It also provides a generous assortment of excerpts from the literature for assignments in analysis. Naturally, the number and type of exercises vary somewhat from unit to unit, depending on the material covered. Thus the exercises for the opening units are intended mainly as a review of the fundamental materials of tonal music. Their purpose is to give the student, as rapidly as possible, a secure grasp of scales, key signatures, intervals, and chords. Although *Harmony & Voice Leading* is not intended as an introduction to fundamentals, there is probably enough material in the workbook for a one-semester course in basic musicianship, if the instructor wishes to use it for that purpose.

Starting with Unit 7, the exercises in both the text and the workbook begin with a series of short drills, called Preliminaries. These form a concentrated review of the most important topics discussed in the unit. The drills are not always easy, but doing them well will give the student the necessary technical foundation for the longer and musically more interesting exercises that follow. If a class falls behind schedule, the instructor would save time by occasionally assigning only the preliminary drills before going on to the next unit. But a steady regimen of these exercises alone is not recommended.

The longer exercises are of various types, but most of them are melodies and basses (both figured and unfigured). It has been more than a century since Arnold Schoenberg decried the use of such exercises, but most harmony textbooks continue to include them, and most instructors continue to assign them. And with very good reason. There is no better way for the student to become aware of the interdependence of the elements of music—how a bass and a soprano combine to form good counterpoint, and how this counterpoint relates to harmonic progression.

A typical homework assignment might well consist of a melody and a bass; for this reason we have interspersed the two rather than separating them. For most units there are two groups of melodies and basses; those in the second group tend to be more difficult than those in the first. We might mention that, once past the beginning stages, students can benefit greatly from working out—and writing out—many solutions to an exercise, trying to determine the good and bad points of each, and deciding which is the best.

The excerpts from the literature, which begin with Unit 8, are suitable for analysis at sight during the classroom hour as well as for homework. As much as possible, students should do more than merely label the chords; they should concentrate on how the chords function, and they should be able to specify the techniques discussed in the unit that are exemplified in each of these excerpts.

E.A.
C.S.
A.C.

Key, Scales, and Modes

Major Scales

1. Given: pitch and scale degree. Write the complete major scale.

SAMPLE

2. Given: note and name of major-scale degree. Write the correct key signature in the space to the right of the note.

SAMPLE

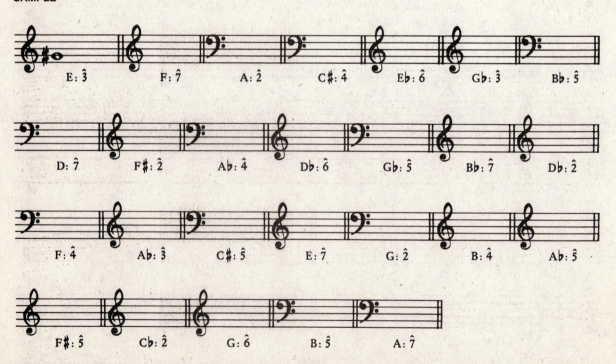

Major Scale Signatures

1. Given: major key signature and note in the key. Provide key and name of
   given scale degree.

SAMPLE

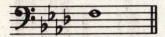

Ab: submediant

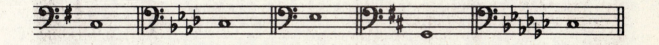

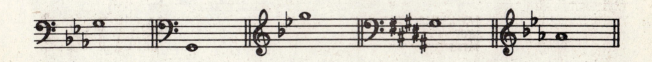

NAME _____

2. Given: note and name of major-scale degree. Write the correct key signature
   in the space to the right of the note.

SAMPLE

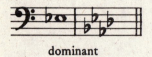

dominant

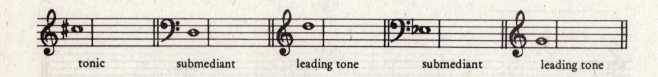

tonic   submediant   leading tone   submediant   leading tone

dominant   submediant   mediant   leading tone   mediant

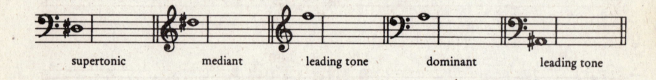

supertonic   mediant   leading tone   dominant   leading tone

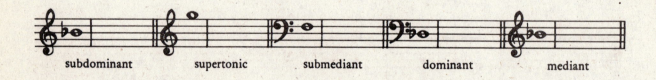

subdominant   supertonic   submediant   dominant   mediant

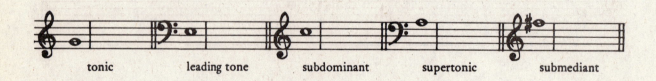

tonic   leading tone   subdominant   supertonic   submediant

Minor Scales

1. Given: pitch and minor-scale degree. Write the complete minor scale specified by these abbreviations: N—natural; H—harmonic; MA—melodic ascending.

NAME _____

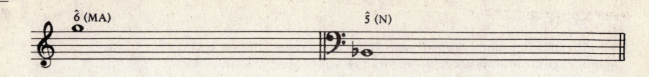

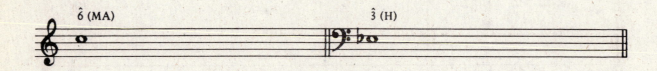

2. Given: minor key and scale degree. Write the correct pitch.

SAMPLE

g#: $\hat{5}$ c#: $\hat{7}$ (N)   f#: $\hat{2}$ bb: $\hat{4}$ c#: $\hat{5}$ f: $\hat{5}$ ab: $\hat{2}$

c#: $\hat{6}$ (MA)   e: $\hat{5}$ g: $\hat{7}$ (H)   b: $\hat{3}$ ab: $\hat{4}$ f#: $\hat{3}$ b: $\hat{7}$ (N)

a: $\hat{6}$ (N)   g: $\hat{2}$ b: $\hat{4}$ e: $\hat{7}$ (H)   f: $\hat{2}$ a: $\hat{4}$ d#: $\hat{6}$ (N)

c: $\hat{5}$ eb: $\hat{7}$ (N)   d: $\hat{4}$ d#: $\hat{3}$ g#: $\hat{2}$

Minor Key Signatures

1. Given: minor key signature and note in the key. Provide the key and the name of given scale degree.

SAMPLE

c#: supertonic
_____

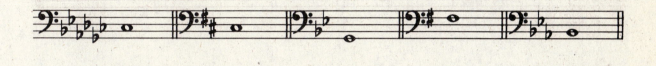

_____   _____   _____   _____   _____

_____   _____   _____   _____   _____

_____   _____   _____   _____   _____

_____   _____   _____   _____   _____

_____   _____   _____   _____   _____

NAME _____

2. Given: note and name of minor-scale degree. Write the correct key signature in the space to the right of the note.

SAMPLE

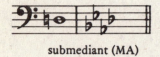

submediant (MA)

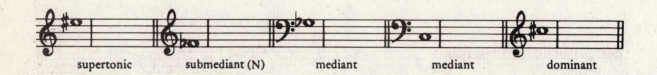

supertonic   submediant (N)   mediant   mediant   dominant

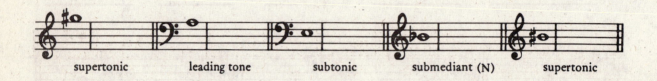

supertonic   leading tone   subtonic   submediant (N)   supertonic

subdominant   leading tone   mediant   subdominant   dominant

subdominant   submediant (MA)   supertonic   leading tone   mediant

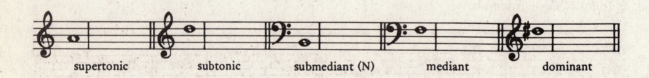

supertonic   subtonic   submediant (N)   mediant   dominant

Intervals

Construction and Identification 1

1. Write intervals above the given notes. Then name the inversions of these
   intervals.

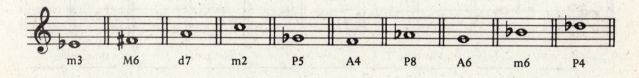

m3   M6   d7   m2   P5   A4   P8   A6   m6   P4

– – – – – – – – – –

inversions

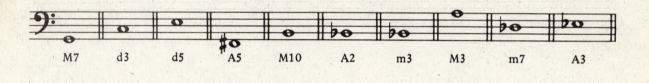

M7   d3   d5   A5   M10   A2   m3   M3   m7   A3

– – – – – – – – – –

inversions

2. Identify these intervals.

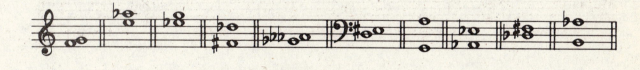

– – – – – – – – – –

10 3. Write intervals below the given notes. Then name the inversions of these intervals.

    m7   M3   d5   m6   P8   d3   M2   P4   M10   A6

___ ___ ___ ___ ___ ___ ___ ___ ___ ___

4. Identify these intervals.

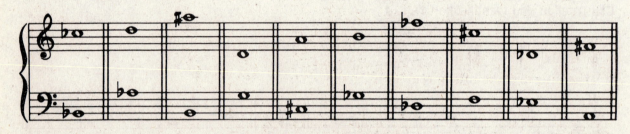

___ ___ ___ ___ ___ ___ ___ ___ ___ ___

1. Write intervals above the given notes.

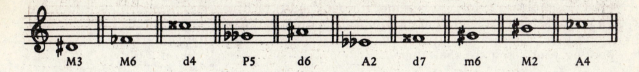

| M3 | M6 | d4 | P5 | d6 | A2 | d7 | m6 | M2 | A4 |

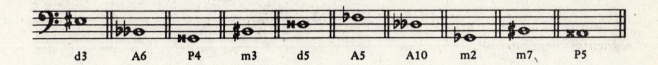

| d3 | A6 | P4 | m3 | d5 | A5 | A10 | m2 | m7 | P5 |

2. Write intervals below the given notes.

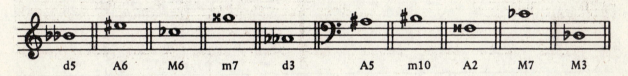

| d5 | A6 | M6 | m7 | d3 | A5 | m10 | A2 | M7 | M3 |

3. Identify these intervals.

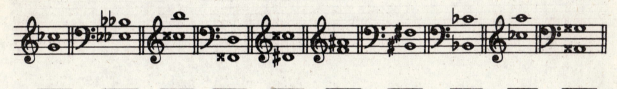

4. Identify these intervals.

NAME _____

12 *Transposition*

These exercises in transposition will test your knowledge both of scale degrees and intervals. Transpose either by *scale degree* (for example, the fifth note in the Mozart example is raised $\hat{4}$; in F♯ minor it would be B♯) or by *melodic interval* (for example, the first interval in the Mozart is a minor 3rd; starting on F♯, the second tone would be A). Try working out each exercise in one way and checking your results by the other.

Transpose these melodies into the keys specified for each.

Ab

B

g#

f

1. Identify these intervals and indicate whether they are consonant (C) or dissonant (D).

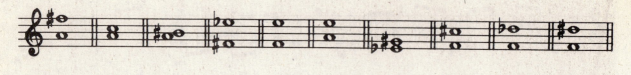

___ ___ ___ ___ ___ ___ ___ ___ ___ ___

2. Write six different consonant intervals above the note A♭. Identify each interval.

___ ___ ___ ___ ___ ___

3. Write twelve different dissonant intervals above D. Identify each interval.

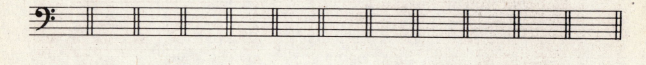

___ ___ ___ ___ ___ ___ ___ ___ ___ ___ ___ ___

4. Name the major keys to which these augmented 4ths and diminished 5ths belong.

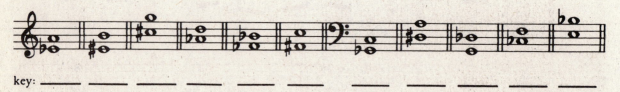

key: ___ ___ ___ ___ ___ ___ ___ ___

5. Name the minor keys to which these augmented 2nds and diminished 7ths belong.

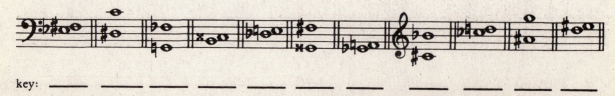

key: ___ ___ ___ ___ ___ ___ ___ ___

Rhythm and Meter

Phrase Groups

Use brackets to indicate the division into phrases in the following excerpts and specify the number of bars in each phrase, as in the sample provided. Many of the phrases are not in normal four- or eight-bar length, and in some of the excerpts the groupings change. In trying to determine where phrases end, look for repeated patterns as well as points of rest. *Warning*: The composers' slurs are signs of articulation and do not necessarily indicate phrase groupings.

SAMPLE

Mozart, Symphony No. 39, K. 543, I

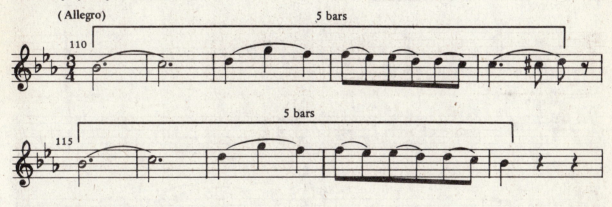

1. Haydn, Symphony No. 104, I

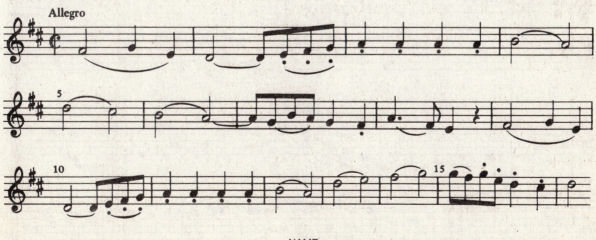

NAME _____

2. Brahms, Variations on a Theme by Haydn, Op. 56a

Theme

3. Beethoven, Piano Sonata, Op. 28, I

4. Beethoven, Piano Sonata, Op. 106, II

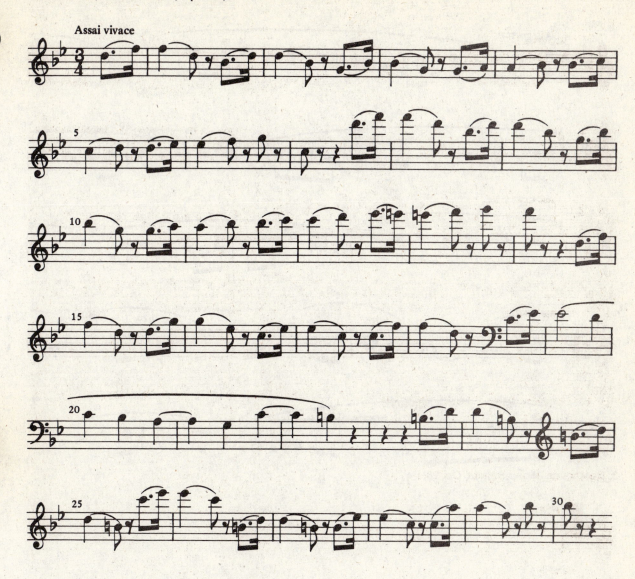

5. Mendelssohn, Song Without Words, Op. 62/1

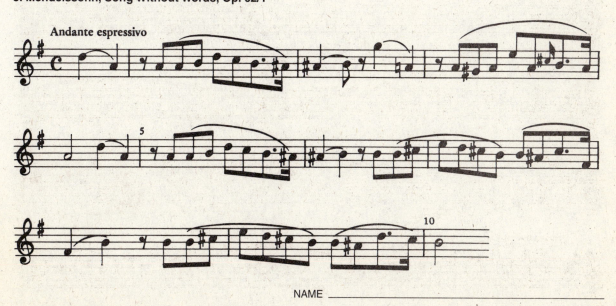

NAME _____

6. Chopin, Mazurka, Op. 59/2

All of the following excerpts contain devices such as syncopation, hemiola, or metric shifts not indicated by the time signature. You must hear them to understand the rhythmic structure of these excerpts. Play or sing each one several times, maintaining a steady beat. If possible, listen to a recording. The following samples demonstrate ways of indicating the devices used.

SAMPLES

(a) Schumann, Albumblätter, Op. 99

(b) Bach, Prelude

(from *English Suite No. 3*, BWV 808)

(c) Strauss, Till Eulenspiegel, Op. 28

NAME _____

7. Bach, Brandenburg Concerto No. 1, III

8. Bach, Well-Tempered Clavier II, Fugue 11

9. Mozart, Symphony No. 41, K. 551 ("Jupiter"), II

NAME _____

10. Beethoven, Piano Sonata, Op. 31/1, I

11. Schumann, Piano Sonata, Op. 22, I

12. Schumann, Symphony No. 3, Op. 97 ("Rhenish"), I

13. Brahms, Symphony No. 1, Op. 68, I

14. Brahms, Violin Sonata, Op. 78, 1

Triads and Seventh Chords

Root-position triads

1. Given: root and quality. Build triads up from the given note.

SAMPLE

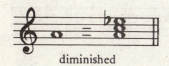

diminished

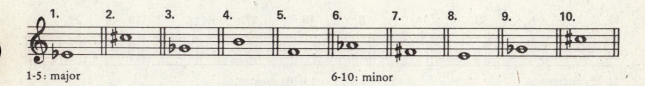

1-5: major   6-10: minor

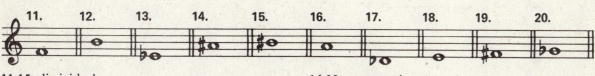

11-15: diminished   16-20: augmented

2. Given: 5th and quality. Build triads down from the given note.

SAMPLE

minor

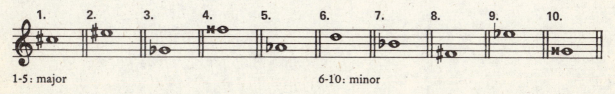

1-5: major   6-10: minor

NAME _____

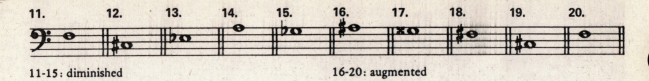

11-15: diminished   16-20: augmented

3. Given: 3rd and quality. Build indicated triads.

SAMPLE

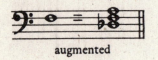

augmented

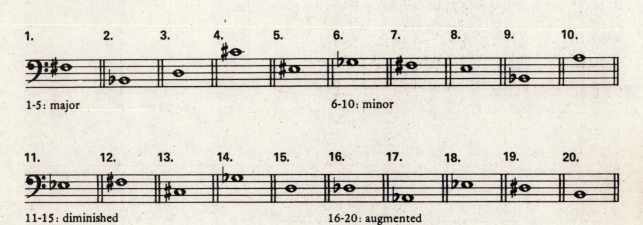

1-5: major   6-10: minor

11-15: diminished   16-20: augmented

1. Name the key defined by each set of triads. Assume major unless some-
   thing contradicts it.

SAMPLE

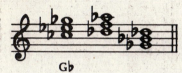

key: _____   _____   _____   _____

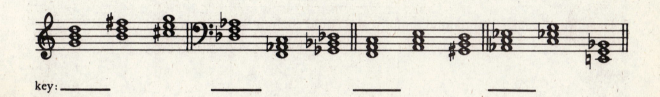

key: _____   _____   _____   _____

key: _____   _____

2. Add *one* triad (*not* the tonic) that will ensure that each set of chords
   belongs to the indicated key.

SAMPLE

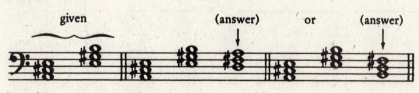

key: A

key: E   c♯   f♯   e

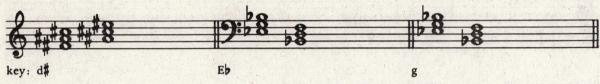

key: C♯   F♯   a♯

key: d♯   E♭   g

3. From which major and natural minor scales could each of these triads be derived?

SAMPLE

major: _____ A, G, D _____

minor: _____ f♯, e, b _____

4. From which harmonic minor scales could each of these triads be derived?

_____ _____ _____ _____

5. From which melodic minor scales could each of these triads be derived?

_____ _____

1. Given: bass. Build triads up.

SAMPLE

m^6_4

M^6_3 m^6_4 d^6_3 A^6_4 m^6_3 M^6_4 A^6_3 d^6_4 M^5_3 d^5_3

2. Given: top voice. Build triads down.

m^6_4

M^6_3 m^6_4 A^5_3 d^6_3 A^6_4 m^6_3 m^5_3 M^6_4 A^6_3 d^6_4

3. With F as the root, build indicated triads.

SAMPLE

F m^5_3

M^6_3 m^6_4 M^5_3 A^5_3 d^6_3 A^6_4 m^6_3 M^6_4 A^6_3 d^6_4

NAME _____

4. Given: key, Roman numeral, and figured bass. Build indicated triads.

SAMPLE

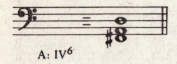

A: IV⁶

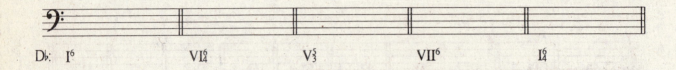

Db: I⁶   VI⁶₄   V⁵₃   VII⁶   I⁶₄

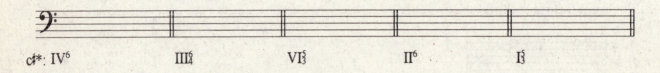

c#*: IV⁶   III⁶₄   VI⁵₃   II⁶   I⁵₃

*use natural minor

5. Identify these triads, giving root, quality, and inversion.

SAMPLE

= Bb A⁶₄

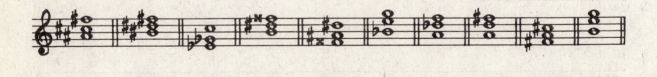

___   ___   ___   ___   ___   ___   ___   ___   ___   ___

1. Build seventh chords according to the quality indicated (M—major; m—
   minor; X—dominant; o—diminished; ∅—half-diminished; A—augmented).

M^7 m^7 X^7 $∅^7$ X^7 o^7 m^7 o^7 A^7 M^7

2. Identify these seventh chords, giving the quality of each.

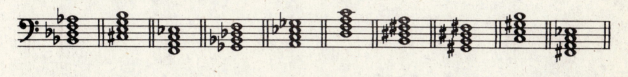

_____ _____ _____ _____ _____ _____ _____ _____ _____ _____

3. Write seventh chords according to the major key and Roman numeral
   given. Name the quality of each chord.

A: II^7 F♯: IV^7 B♭: VI^7 E♭: III^7 D♭: I^7 E: III^7 G♭: V^7 A♭: IV^7 C♯: II^7 B: VI^7

_____ _____ _____ _____ _____ _____ _____ _____ _____ _____

NAME _____

1. Identify, giving root, quality, and figured-bass symbol.

SAMPLE

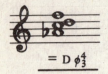

= D ø$^4_3$

2. Given: root, quality, and inversion. Write indicated chords.

SAMPLE

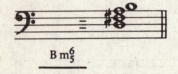

B m$^6_5$

Ab m$^4_3$ E M$^6_5$ B X^7 F M$^4_2$ G ø$^4_3$ D# o$^6_5$ C# m$^4_2$ D ⁶^7 G# m$^4_3$ A# o$^6_5$

3. Write dominant seventh chords on the notes given. Then indicate the major key in which each chord occurs.

SAMPLE

$^6_5$ key: E

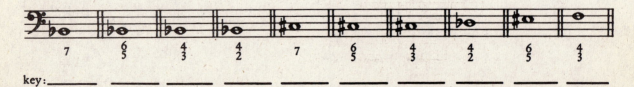

7    $^6_5$ $^4_3$ $^4_2$ 7 $^6_5$ $^4_3$ $^4_2$ $^6_5$ $^4_3$

key: _____ _____ _____ _____ _____ _____ _____ _____ _____ _____

4. Write diminished seventh chords on the given notes. Then indicate the
   harmonic minor scale from which each chord would be derived.

SAMPLE

    7   key: **b**

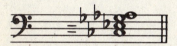

    7   ⁶₅   ⁴₃   ⁴₂   7   ⁶₅   ⁴₃   ⁴₂   7   ⁴₂

key: _____ _____ _____ _____ _____ _____ _____ _____ _____ _____

5. Write the indicated chords, then name the quality of each.

SAMPLE

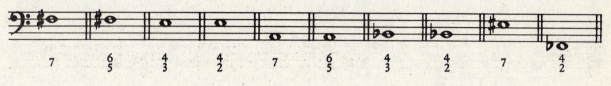

G♭ : II⁶₅ quality: _____**m**_____

A♭: IV⁶₅   G: II⁴₃   E: VII⁴₂   A: VI⁴₂   F: II⁶₅   D: VII⁷   F♯: II⁴₂   B♭: VI⁴₃   B: IV⁷   G: I⁴₃

quality: _____ _____ _____ _____ _____ _____ _____ _____ _____ _____

Introduction to Counterpoint

These exercises provide material for writing cantus firmi and counterpoints in all five species. We strongly recommend, however, writing more than two solutions for each species. For additional practice, draw from among the other cantus firmi listed here or from those provided at the conclusion of Unit 5 in the text. Assignment No. 12 can be used as a final project for all five species.

Counterpoint Exercise No. 1: Cantus Firmus

Write two cantus firmi, one in the major and one in the minor mode.
The length should be from 9 to 14 notes.

a minor

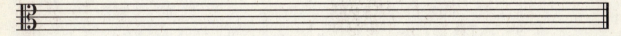

F major

36   Counterpoint Exercise No. 2: First-species counterpoint

Write a first-species counterpoint above the CF. Be sure to raise scale degree $\hat{7}$ at the cadence.

Counterpoint Exercise No. 3: First-species counterpoint

Write a first-species counterpoint below the CF.

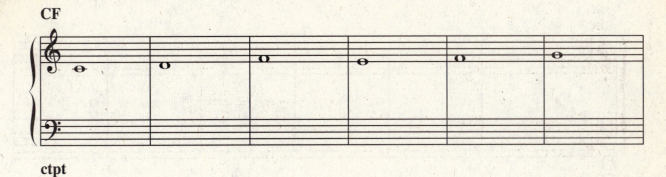

CF

ctpt

38   *Counterpoint Exercise No. 4: Second-species counterpoint*

Write a second-species counterpoint above the CF.

ctpt

CF

Counterpoint Exercise No. 5: Second-species counterpoint

Write a second-species counterpoint below the CF.

40 *Counterpoint Exercise No. 6: Third-species counterpoint*

Write a third-species counterpoint above the CF.

ctpt

CF

Counterpoint Exercise No. 7: Third-species counterpoint

Write a third-species counterpoint below the CF.

CF

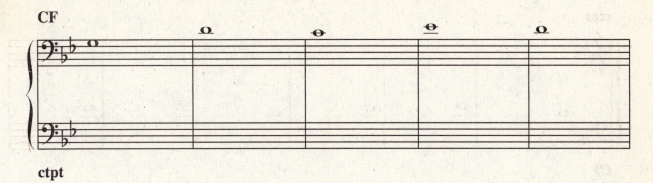

ctpt

42   *Counterpoint Exercise No. 8: Fourth-species counterpoint*

Write a fourth-species counterpoint above the CF.

ctpt

CF

Counterpoint Exercise No. 9: Fourth-species counterpoint

Write a fourth-species counterpoint below the CF.

CF

ctpt

Counterpoint Exercise No. 10: Fifth-species counterpoint

Write a fifth-species counterpoint above the CF.

Counterpoint Exercise No. 11: Fifth-species counterpoint

Write a fifth-species counterpoint below the CF.

CF

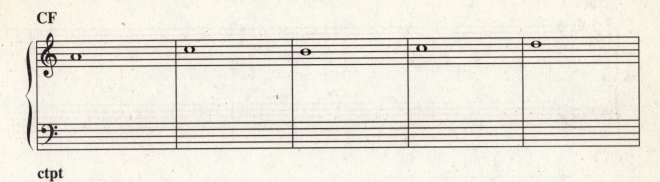

ctpt

Assignment No. 12: Final Project

A counterpoint exercise in open score. Write counterpoints in all five species
above and below the given cantus firmus.

UNIT 6

Procedures of Four-Part Writing

1 bottom up.
2. Identify the Root
3. Id the inversion
4. system/quality

Chord Identification

Triads

1. (a) Identify the following triads, giving root, quality (M, m, A, or d), and inversion.
   (b) Assuming a key signature with no sharps or flats, write the correct figured-bass symbols for these chords.

SAMPLE

(a) Ab M$^6_3$ C#   Bb $^6_3$ Eb Aug   Gmin

(b) b^6_b

2. Given: major key signature. Supply key, Roman numeral, and figured bass.

SAMPLE

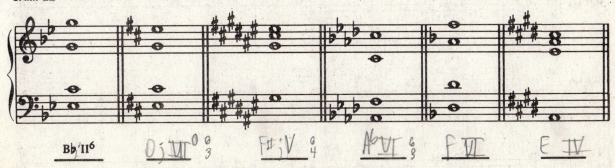

Bb II^6 Db VI$^{00}_3$ F# V$^0_4$ Ab VI$^6_3$ F VII   E IV

NAME

___ ___ ___ ___ ___ ___ ___ ___

Seventh Chords

3. (a) Identify the following seventh chords, giving root, quality (M, m, X, o, ∅, A, or m/M) and inversion.
   (b) Assuming a key signature with no sharps or flats, write the correct figured-bass symbols for these chords.

SAMPLE

(a)   Ab X$^6_5$ ___ ___ ___ ___ ___ ___ ___ ___

(b) $^{b6}_{b5}$ ___ ___ ___ ___ ___ ___ ___ ___
      $_b$

4. Given: major key signature. Supply key, Roman numeral, and figured bass.

SAMPLE

E IV$^6_5$ ___ ___ ___ ___ ___

___ ___ ___ ___ ___

Chord Construction 1

Given: key and Roman numeral; chord spacing (open or close or keyboard style); doubling. Construct four-voice chords as indicated, adding the appropriate key signature. All chords should be complete unless an incomplete chord is specified.

leading tone: resolve up by step · resolve down by step

Close : don't skip chord tones in between

SAMPLE

key and chord: C♯: III	Ab: II	c♯: VI	D: VII	g: I
spacing: open	open	close	open	close
doubling: root	root	root	3rd	root

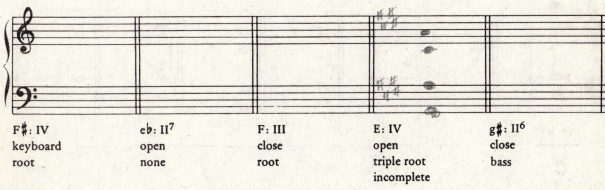

F♯: IV	eb: II⁷	F: III	E: IV	g♯: II⁶
keyboard	open	close	open	close
root	none	root	triple root incomplete	bass

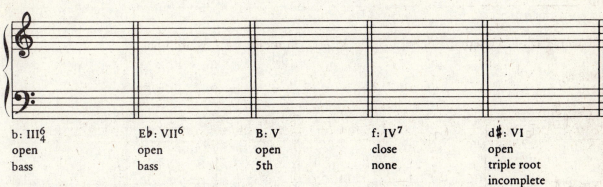

b: III$^6_4$	Eb: VII⁶	B: V	f: IV⁷	d♯: VI
open	open	open	close	open
bass	bass	5th	none	triple root incomplete

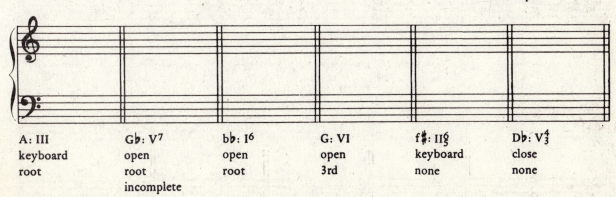

A: III	Gb: V⁷	bb: I⁶	G: VI	f♯: II$^6_5$	Db: V$^4_3$
keyboard	open	open	open	keyboard	close
root	root incomplete	root	3rd	none	none

NAME _____

50 *Chord Construction 2*

Indicate mistakes of spacing, doubling, vocal range, and so on, in the chords. (Not all of them are wrong.) Write corrected versions of the same chords in the space next to each.

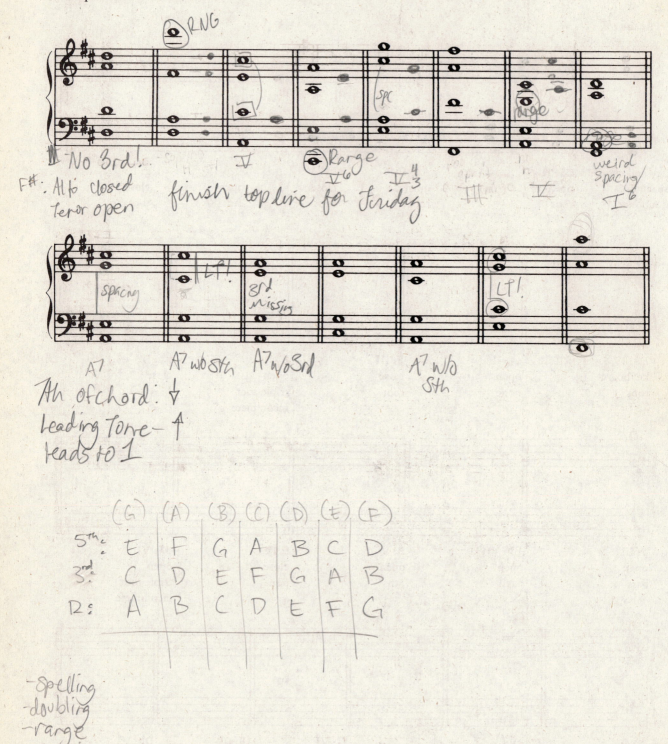

RNG

No 3rd!

F#: Alto closed
Tenor open

finish top line for Friday

Range
V6

III

IV

weird
spacing
I6

spacing

A7

A7 w/o 5th

A7 w/o 3rd

A7 w/o
5th

7th of chord: ↓
Leading Tone — ↑
leads to 1

	(G)	(A)	(B)	(C)	(D)	(E)	(F)
5th:	E	F	G	A	B	C	D
3rd:	C	D	E	F	G	A	B
R:	A	B	C	D	E	F	G

-spelling
-doubling
-range
-spacing

Voice Leading

Indicate the mistakes of voice leading and chord construction in the following
exercises, using the same procedure as in the text examples.

1.

2.

NAME _____

Melodic Fragments (I, V, and V⁷)

Harmonize the melodic fragments below using, I, V, and, wherever possible, V^7. Some should be harmonized twice—once in major and once in the relative minor (same notes but different scale degrees).

SOLUTIONS

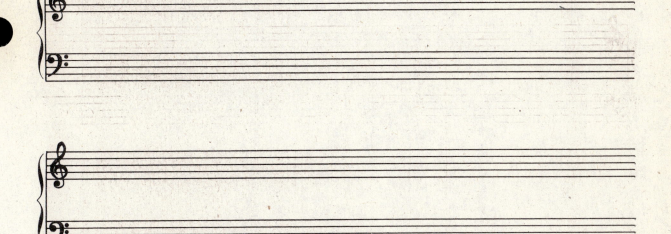

I⁶, V⁶, and VII⁶

Preliminaries

Melodic and Figured-Bass Fragments (Including I⁶ and V⁶)

1. Set the following for four voices, using I, V, V⁷, I⁶, and V⁶ only. No VII⁶!
   When setting the melodic fragments, be sure to use I⁶ and V⁶ where
   appropriate.

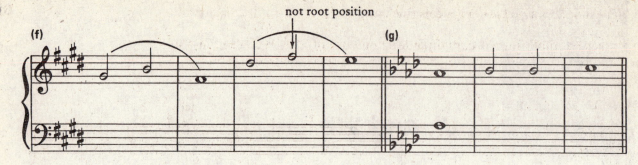

not root position

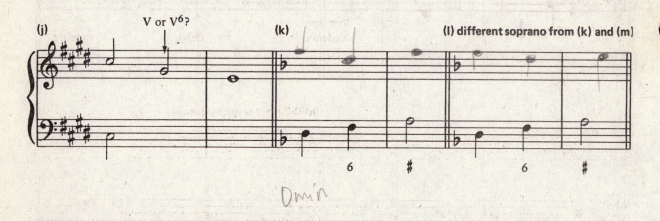

(i) set differently from (h)

cadence

cadence

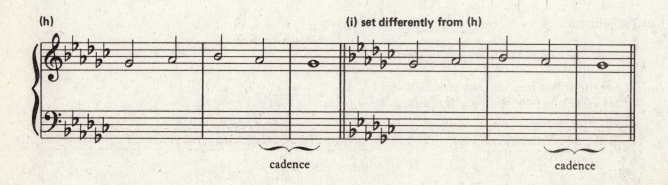

V or V⁶?

(l) different soprano from (k) and (m)

5. **Melody and figured bass.** Use voice exchanges where appropriate, and use at least one VII^6 in the first phrase.

6. **Chorale melody.** Harmonize *all* the notes.

7. **Chorale melody.** Harmonize *all* the notes.

NAME _____

Study and Analysis

In addition to labeling each chord (Roman numeral and figure), be able to explain the *function* of each chord. How long does the tonic chord at the beginning of bar 4 last?

L'Écho   (Anon.)

Melodies and Basses 2

1. **Figured bass.** Label the function of each *active* soprano tone.

2. **Melody.** Octaves by contrary motion OK in final cadence.

3. **Unfigured bass.**

4. **Melody.**

NAME _____

68 *Study and Analysis*

Besides labeling the chords, indicate the function of all nontonic chords.

1. Beethoven, Piano Sonata, Op. 26, I

2. Mendelssohn, Symphony No. 4, Op. 90 ("Italian"), III

Which chord is expanded here?

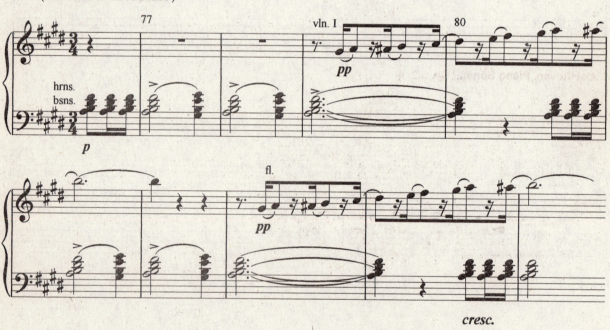

3. Bach, Chorale 1

4. Schumann, Arabesque, Op. 18

5. Beethoven, Piano Sonata, Op. 2/2, II

6. Beethoven, Piano Sonata, Op. 10/3, I

NAME _____

70   **7. Schubert, Der Neugierige** (The Curious One)   (from *Die schöne Mullerin*, D. 795)

Ich fra - ge kei - ne Blu - me, ich fra - ge kei - nen Stern;

Translation: I ask no flower, I ask no star;

Longer Assignments

Melodies and Basses 1

1. **Figured bass.**

2. **Melody**.

3. **Unfigured bass**. Remember that in all unfigured basses from this point on, where the bass is $\hat{2}$ or $\hat{4}$, you have to decide whether to use *dominant* or *intermediate* harmony. Set in keyboard style and add appropriate figures for the bass. What is the best soprano note for the first beat of bar 2?

4. **Unfigured bass and melody**.

NAME _____

1. Given: outer voices. Fill in inner parts and provide figures for the bass. Be
   able to explain the function of each chord.

2. **Unfigured bass**. What melodic line is suggested by the first four notes of
   this bass?

3. **Melody**. The phrase beginning measure 5 starts with an incomplete
   progression.

4. **Melody.**

1. Beethoven, Piano Concerto No. 1, Op. 15, I

What are the main soprano notes in measures 107, 109, and 111?

2. Mozart, Violin Sonata, K. 377, II

3. Mozart, Violin Sonata, K. 296, 1

Would the harmony always be complete if the violin part were omitted?

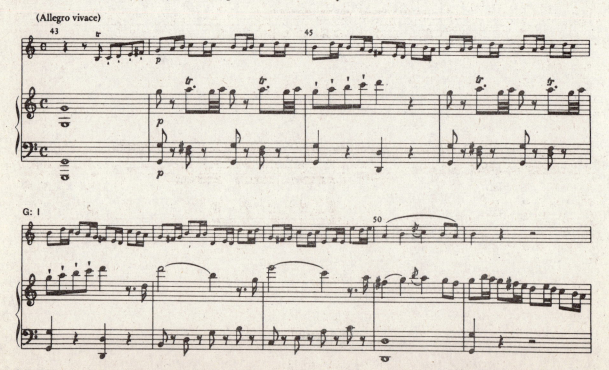

4. Beethoven, Piano Concerto, Op. 58, I

5. Mozart, Piano Sonata, K. 310, I

NAME _____

3. **Melody.** Use the cadential $\frac{6}{4}$ on the starred notes.

bass: 𝅗𝅥.

4. **Unfigured bass.** Before setting this exercise for four voices, study the bass line and determine the *function* of each note. Then provide figures for the bass, looking for opportunities to use the cadential $\frac{6}{4}$. In some cases, there may be more than one correct possibility—in addition to some very incorrect ones. Work out the soprano next and, finally, fill in the inner voices.

NAME _____

1. Mozart, An Chloë, K. 524

Wenn die Lieb aus dei-nen blau - en, hel - len,

off - nen Au-gen sieht, und für Lust, hin-ein zu schau - en, mir's ___ im ___

Her-zen klopft und _ glüht,

Translation:
When love gazes from your blue, bright, open eyes,
and with joy of gazing into them my heart throbs
and glows, . . .

2. Mozart, Violin Sonata, K. 380, I

What is the function of the chord in bar 2? Study the relation between the phrase groupings and harmonic progression. What is the justification for repeating the chord succession of bars 7–8, in bars 9–10, and 11–12? (Look at the violin part.)

NAME _____

84   3. Haydn, Symphony No. 83 ("La Poule"), I

How many large-scale harmonic progressions are there in this excerpt? Is there an overlap between phrases? Are any chords extended beyond what would seem to be their normal length?

one chord or two?

Longer Assignments

Melodies and Basses 1

1. Melody.

VI   VI   VI

2. Unfigured bass.

Em   IV⁶   I   V   IV   V   I   IV⁶   I   IV   I⁶   IV⁶   IV   V   I

3. Melody.

bass arpeggio

4. Figured bass.

1. **Outer voices** (unfigured bass).

2. **Melody.**

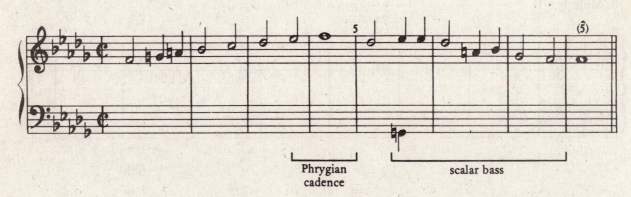

Phrygian
cadence

scalar bass

3. Unfigured bass.

1. Mahler, Symphony No. 2, IV

Translation: Oh little red rose!

2. Mozart, Piano Sonata, K. 311, II

3. Beethoven, Piano Sonata, Op. 10/1, II

How many phrases are there, and how do they relate to one another? Do you hear the A♭ chord in bar 7 as a goal tonic, or as incidental to another, larger progression? If so, to what progression?

4. Handel, Concerto Grosso, Op. 3/2, I

Grave

5. Bach, Chorale 56

What is the function of the tied F♯ in bar 2, beat 1?

NAME _____

6. Mozart, Piano Sonata, K. 311, I

A:

7. Mozart, Violin Sonata, K. 379, I

8. Haydn, Piano Sonata, Hob. XVI/37, III

Supertonic and Subdominant Seventh Chords

Preliminaries

Melodic Fragments

Set for four voices, using a position of II^7 or IV^7 whenever possible. (It's not always possible.)

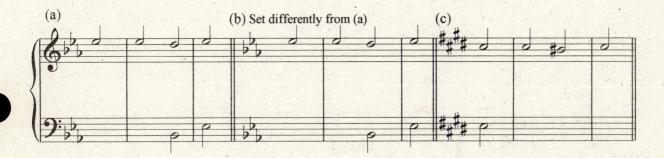

(a)   (b) Set differently from (a)   (c)

(d)   (e)   (f) Is supertonic 7th possible?

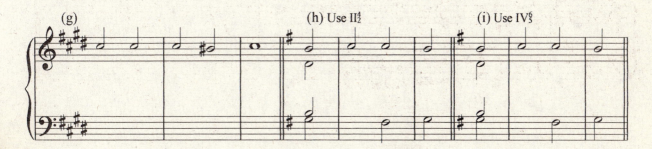

(g)   (h) Use II$^4_2$ (i) Use IV$^6_5$

NAME _____

Longer Assignments

Melodies and Basses 1

1. **Unfigured bass**. Use II^7, II^6_5, or II^4_2 for the starred notes.

2. **Melody**. Use keyboard style. Use IV^7 twice and IV^6_5 *once* for the starred notes.

scalar bass

3. **Figured bass**. Warning! Be careful not to write parallel 5ths in bar 2!

NAME _____

1. **Melody.** Set in four-part keyboard style. Use II^7 or an inversion of II^7 for
   the starred notes.

no cadence!

2. **Figured bass.**

3. **Melody**. Fermatas indicate cadential points.

4. **Melody**. * = supertonic or subdominant 7ths or their inversions.
Hint: Insofar as possible, keep the voices in close position during the 1st phrase.

NAME _____

1. Beethoven, Kyrie   (from *Missa Solemnis*, Op. 123)

2. Mozart, String Quartet, K. 428, III

Study the preparation and resolution of the dissonance of the chord in bar 2.
Is the dissonance *heard* as unprepared? Why not? Where does it resolve?

3. Mozart, String Quartet, K. 458, I.

What is the form of this excerpt? How does the dissonance of bar 3, the fifth eighth note, come about? (Look at the entire measure.)

4. Schumann, from Album for the Young, Op. 68

Where does the C in the "alto" of bar 1 resolve?

NAME _____

5. Bach, Little Prelude No. 5, BWV 928

How does the first half of bar 20 relate to the second half?

6. Bach, Chorale 72 Explain the leaps in the tenor voice.

7. Bach, Well-Tempered Clavier II, Figure 16

8. Mozart, The Magic Flute, K. 620: Act I, Finale

Translation: As soon as the hand of friendship leads you into the sanctuary, to the eternal bond.

Other Uses of IV, IV⁶, and VI

Preliminaries

Melodic Fragments and Unfigured Basses

use disjunct bass

102 *Longer Assignments*

Melodies and Basses 1

1. **Melody**.

deceptive cadence

bass: ♩ ♩ ♩

2. **Melody**. Add accidentals where needed, including the soprano voice.
There should be a plagal cadence at the end.

not I!

bass: ♩ ♩ ♩

3. Melody and unfigured bass.

4. Figured bass. Keyboard style is possible.

Andante con moto

1. Melody.

not I!

bass descends in 3rds

bass:

2. Figured bass. Use keyboard style.

3. Melody.

dissonant chord   not I

bass:

overlap OK

bass:

4. Melody.

overlap OK

5

NAME _____

5. **Folksong**. Write an accompaniment in four voices, using IV⁶ more than once. Apparent octaves and unisons between the three upper voices of the accompaniment and the solo line are permissible.

(German)

6. **Folksong, "La Bergère."** Make a different harmonization of the bracketed repeated phrase in bars 9–10 so that the final tonic sounds really final. As with the previous folksong, apparent octaves and unisons between the three upper voices of the accompaniment and the solo line are permissible.

(French)

1. Schumann, Soldatenmarsch
(from *Album for the Young,* Op. 68)

Discuss the relationship between the outer voices.

2. Mozart, Violin Sonata, K. 377, III

3. Bach, Chorale 73

4. Beethoven, Symphony No. 6, Op. 68 ("Pastorale"), V

5. Handel, Concerto Grosso, Op. 6/1, II

* = (♯) IV⁷

NAME _____

6. Mozart, Piano Sonata, K. 279, II

7. Handel, "Lift Up Your Heads"

is the King of glo - ry,   of glo - ry.

is the King of glo - ry,   of glo - ry.

is the King of glo - ry,   of glo - ry.

is the King of glo - ry,   of glo - ry.

8. Bach, Well-Tempered Clavier I, Fugue 17

9. Bach, Prelude (from Prelude and Fugue, BWV 544)

Organ

NAME _____

10. Beethoven, "Waldstein" Sonata, Op. 53, I

V as a Key Area

Preliminaries

Short Bass Lines

For the most part these basses are unfigured. In each exercise, label the two key areas and indicate the pivot chord(s). Be sure you plan the soprano voice so that the cadences will make sense.

(a) (b)

(c) (d)

= B : IV   4+/2

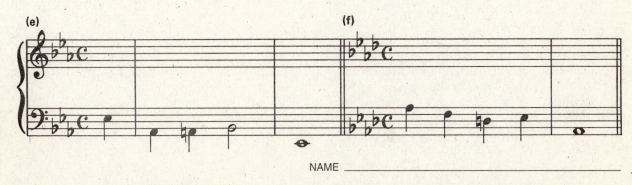

(e) (f)

(g)

(h)

Longer Assignments

1. **Unfigured bass**. Outer voices given.

* = neighbor; don't harmonize.

2. **Figured bass**. Use keyboard style.

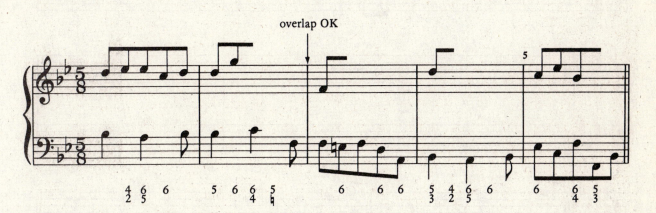

116   3. **Folksong, "Rinaldo Rinaldini".**
The accompaniment can have a free and varied chordal rhythm: some-
times a chord might last through a whole bar, while at other times the
chords will change on every beat.

4. Folksong, "Der Schlossergesell" (The Journeyman Locksmith)

NAME _____

118   5. **Türk, March (adapted).**
Set in free keyboard style, as in bars 1–2. The number of voices may
change, and octaves may be added to the bass occasionally for emphasis.

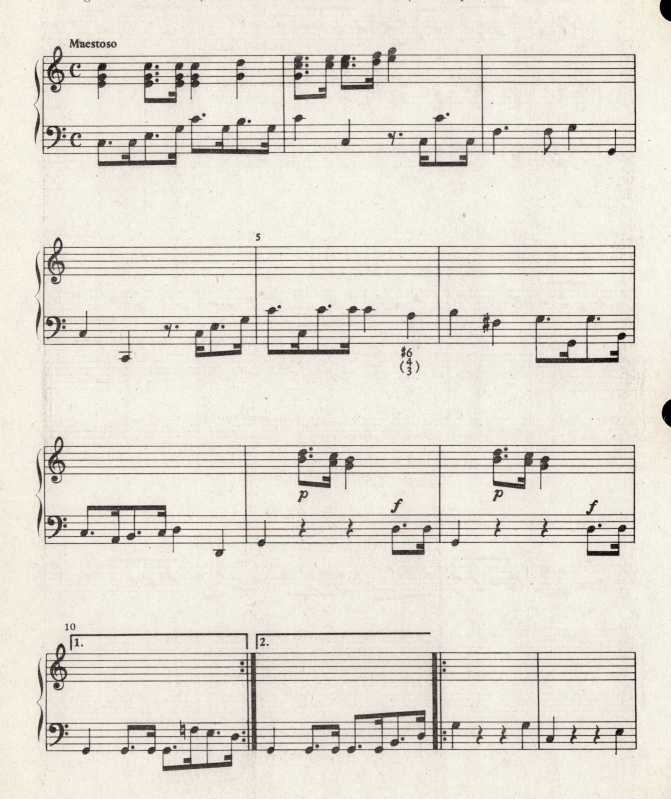

120   6. **For String Quartet.**
Be able to explain the form. Explain the 10-bar period at the beginning.

avoid authentic
cadence

Project: The Duchess's Lullaby (Lewis Carroll)

Complete the melody and provide a piano accompaniment. This part that is given forms an antecedent phrase that modulates to V. Write a consequent phrase that sets the remainder of the poem (given at the bottom of the next page), but this time ending in the tonic (the beginning of the consequent should be the same as the antecedent). This humorous "anti-lullaby" should be everything that a real lullaby is not: slashing, fortissimo chords marking the beats, and a march-like tune instead of gentle, rocking rhythms and soft dynamics. The poem comes from the "Pig and Pepper" chapter of *Alice in Wonderland,* and it is sung by the Duchess to a baby boy who will soon turn into a pig. Your setting (and any performance of the song) should reflect the crazy and chaotic atmosphere of the Duchess's kitchen, where the air is saturated with pepper, and the ferocious and violent cook keeps throwing pots, pans, and dishes at everyone in sight.

Note: If you have never read the two Alice books, get them immediately and remedy this deficiency (even if it means skimping on your theory homework for a few days).

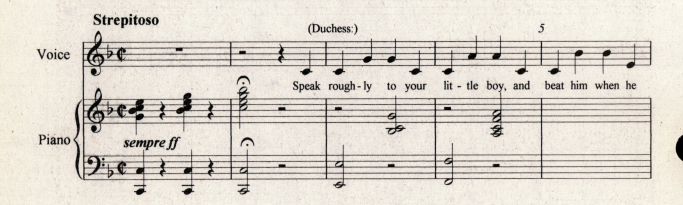

(Duchess, Cook, and Baby:)

Wow! wow! wow!

I speak se-vere-ly to my boy, And beat him when he sneez-es
For he can tho-rough-ly enjoy the pep-per when he pleas-es.
Wow! wow! wow!

NAME _____

In studying these examples, consider how the modulations or tonicizations relate to the form of the piece.

1. Mozart, "Die kleine Spinnerin," K. 531

"Was spinnst du?" frag-te Nachbars Fritz, als

er uns jüngst be - such - te; "dein Räd - chen läuft ja wie der Blitz, sag' an, wo - zu dies fruch - te; komm

lie - ber her in un - ser Spiel!" "Herr Fritz, das lass' ich blei - ben; ich kann mir, wenn er's wis - sen will, so

auch die Zeit ver - trei - ben, so auch die Zeit ver - trei - ben."

*VII°⁷ of V

Translation: "What are you spinning?" asked our neighbor Fritz when he visited us recently; "your spinning wheel runs like lightning; tell me, what's the good of it? Come out and play with us instead!"

"Herr Fritz, I can do without that; if you really want to know, I can kill time, too."

NAME _____

Translation: In a bright little brook, with joyous speed, the playful trout darted like an arrow. I stood on the bank and, happily at rest, watched the lively fish bathe in the clear brook.

130 Project: Handel, "Và godendo"

This excerpt from Handel's opera *Serse* is an assignment that combines analysis and writing. It is presented here as in the original score: voice accompanied by continuo (unfigured bass), and orchestral interludes (violin and flute). Complete the accompaniment by adding three voices above the bass and by adding *one* voice between the violin and flute. In your analysis, note how the tonicized V relates to the form of the excerpt.

E tra____ l'er - be

basses

con on - de chia - re lie - to al - ma - re cor - ren - do và,___

= ♩.

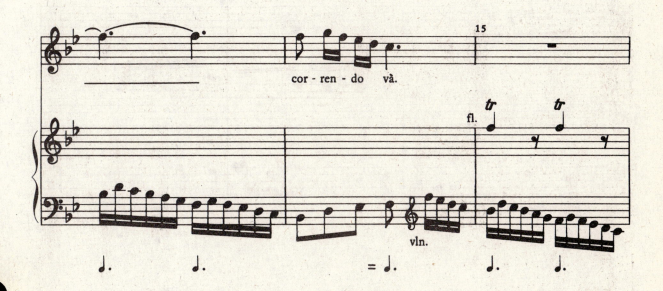

cor - ren - do và.

fl. *tr* *tr*

vln.

♩. ♩. = ♩. ♩. ♩.

Translation: Merrily and gracefully flows the freely running brook. And with limpid waves, it rushes joyously through the grass to the sea.

III and VII

Preliminaries

Bass-Line Fragments with III

Use III, but not VII, in the following exercises. Write a different soprano for each of the repeated bass lines. These basses are mostly unfigured.

134   **Figured-Bass Fragments with III and VII**

Use both III and natural VII in this group of exercises. Again, do not repeat a
soprano over a repeated bass.

Longer Assignments

Melodies and Basses with III

Use III, but not VII, in the following settings.

1. **Figured bass.**

2. **Melody.**

* The 16ths need not be harmonized.

NAME _____

136   3. **Figured bass**. Set in keyboard style.

4. **Melody.**

5. **Folksong.** When the melody skips down, the right hand of the accompaniment can stay above it.

(English)

NAME _____

1. **Unfigured bass**.

*The 16ths are figuration; sustain the upper voices.

2. **Melody (adapted from Chopin)**. Either a four-voice or a piano setting is possible. Use two different chords per measure.

3. Melody.

III _____

_____ *don't harmonize

1. Schumann, Symphonic Etudes, Op. 13, Etude 9

(Presto possibile)

2. Bach, Geistliche Lieder, No. 45

3. Bach, Chorale 62 (adapted)

4. Bach, Geistliche Lieder, No. 53

The b♭ of measure 6 is an accented passing tone; the $\frac{5}{2}$ will become a $\frac{6}{3}$ over the a.

Ihr Ge - stirn, ihr ho - hen__ Lüf - te, und du,__ lich - tes Fir - ma - ment,
tie - fes Rund, ihr dunk - len__ Klüf - te, die der__ Wi - der - schall zer - trennt,

jauch - zet____ fröh - lich, lasst das Sin - gen____ itzt bis durch_ die Wol - ken_ drin - gen.

Translation: Bright stars, dark chasms, shout with joy,
let your singing reach the clouds.

5. Mozart, "Porgi amor"   (from *Marriage of Figaro*, K. 492)

Contessa

Por - gi a - mor qual - che ri - sto - ro

orchestral reduction

al mio duo - lo, a' miei - so - spir

Translation: Deliver, love, some solace to my grief, to my sighs . . .

6. Beethoven, Bagatelle, Op. 33/2

$\frac{5}{3}$-Chord Techniques

Because exercises using root-position chords alone are necessarily artificial, the writing assignments for this unit consist only of short drills and one longer exercise using V in minor as a minor triad. But, needless to say, the techniques you will practice in this unit are important for your written work in all subsequent units.

Preliminaries

1. **Bass-line fragments**.

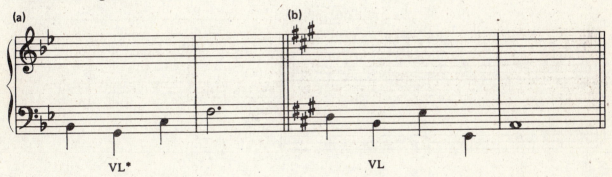

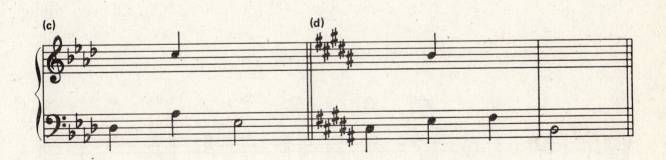

*VL = voice-leading chord

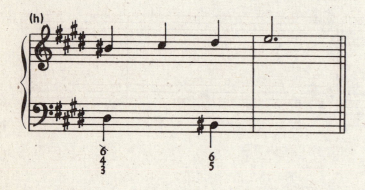

2. Supply the missing chord, using root-position triads only.

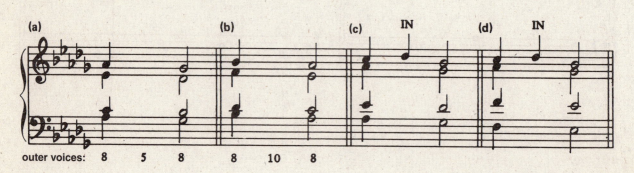

outer voices: 8   5   8   8   10   8

146 *Longer Assignment*

Sarabande

Set in free keyboard style, using V as a minor triad where appropriate. The number of voices may change as necessary.

Indicate the function of the starred chords in the first five excerpts.

1. Bach, Chorale 296

2. Bach, Chorale 217

3. Beethoven, Piano Sonata, Op. 14/1, II

4. Schubert, Piano Sonata, D. 850, III

5. Chopin, Prelude, Op. 28/9

NAME _____

6. Beethoven, Piano Sonata, Op. 2/2, II

What unifies the chord succession in this excerpt?

UNIT 18

Diatonic Sequences

Preliminaries

Melody and Bass-Line Fragments

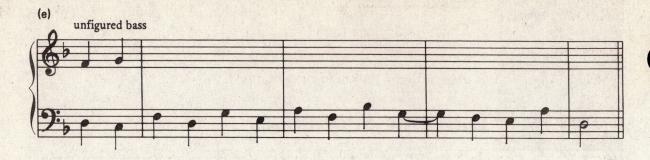

(e) unfigured bass

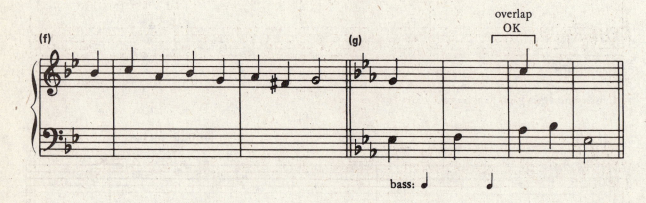

(f) (g) overlap OK

bass:

(h) different bass overlap OK (i)

bass:

Longer Assignments

Melodies and Bass

1. **Melody**. Use $\frac{5}{3}$ chords only (with the indicated exception).

2. **Melody**.

NAME _____

154   3. **Figured bass**. The opening sequential passage incorporates a technique
   discussed in Units 16 and 17: giving consonant support to a passing tone.

Prelude

Complete the two-voice keyboard setting. In two voices, you should generally
avoid perfect intervals on strong beats, except at cadences or other points of
emphasis. Which measures demonstrate *Fortspinnung*?

NAME _____

156   Gavotte

Complete in a free keyboard setting, using three and four voices as needed.
The bass is unfigured. Don't harmonize the starred notes.

Melody and Incomplete Unfigured Bass

1. Handel

(from Handel's *Serse*, 1738)

Complete the accompaniment, and add a bass line to bars 9 and 29–34.

NAME _____

a - na, tu - li - pa - na, gel - so - mi - na,

ah! chi vo - ler fio - ra di bel - la giar -

di - na, chi vo - ler fio - ra di bel - la giar - di - na!

Translation: Who wants to buy flowers from the beautiful garden—hyacinths, passion flowers, tulips, jasmine!

Study and Analysis

Identify the type of sequence and indicate how the sequence functions in a larger context. In addition, a valuable exercise would be to reduce some or all these excerpts to their basic sequential pattern. See the reduction following excerpt no. 11.

1. Corelli, Trio Sonata, Op. 1/3, Allegro

A: I

2. Corelli, Trio Sonata, Op. 1/10, Allegro

g: III

tonicizes what?

3. Corelli, Trio Sonata, Op. 2/11, Allemande

NAME _____

4. Handel, Adagio   (from Harpsichord Suite No. 2)

5. Bach, Two-Part Invention No. 12, BWV 873

6. Bach, Flute Sonata in C, BWV 1033, I

7. Handel, "Và godendo" (from *Serse*)

(The text is the same as that of the project at the end of Unit 15.)

8. Haydn, Symphony No. 103, I (bars 50–59, strings only)

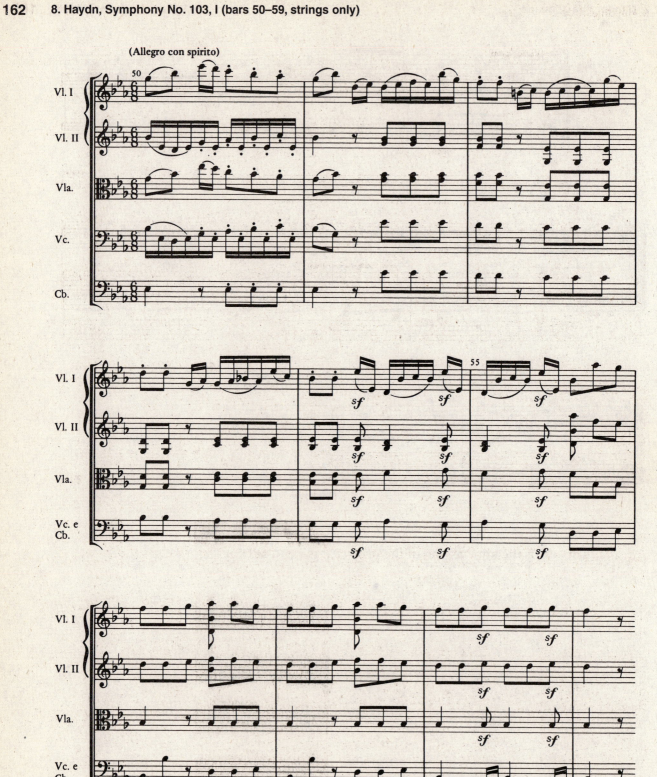

9. Haydn, Credo   (from *Heiligmesse*, 1796)

(from *Don Giovanni*, K. 527)

Translation: Dear lady, this is the list of the beautiful women my master has loved, a list that I have compiled, look at it, read it with me.

166   **11. Beethoven, Piano Sonata, Op. 28, IV**

Continue the reduction that begins in (b). Change from 3 voices to 4 where necessary.

(b) reduction

12. Schubert, Two Dances, D. 365

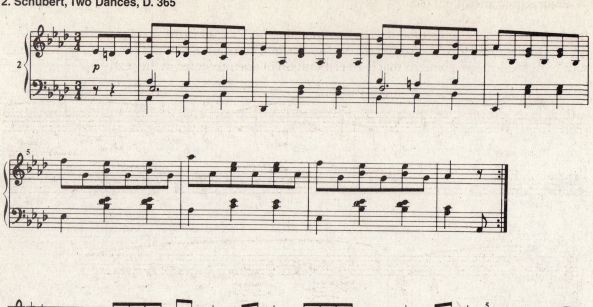

13. Chopin, Etude, Op. 25/9

14. Brahms, Romanze, Op. 118/5

Brahms disguises the sequential bass by manipulating both register (the first bass note) and rhythm. Once you've sketched a "normalized" version of this bass (and soprano), you will see a pattern that is an elaboration of one presented in the text.

15. Beethoven, Symphony No. 5, Op. 67, I (bars 439–469)

How is the material beginning in bar 440 different from the sequences discussed in this unit? Is there a sequence that *does* illustrate a pattern presented in the text?

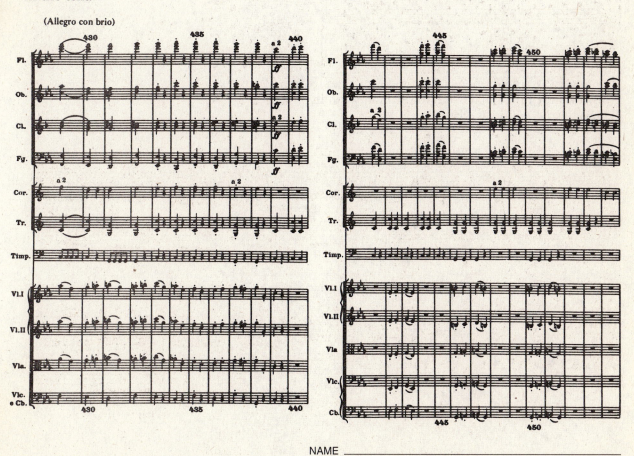

NAME _____

Clarinets in B♭ sound one whole step lower than written.
Horns in E♭ sound a major 6th lower than written.
Trumpets in C sound as written.

UNIT 19

$\frac{6}{3}$ - Chord Techniques

Preliminaries

The outer voices are given. Except for the few figures given, the bass should be regarded as unfigured. Add the inner voices, using $\frac{6}{3}$ chords wherever appropriate.

add accidentals where needed

NAME _____

19

171

Longer Assignments

Melodies and Basses

1. **Figured bass** (adapted from Handel).
   In this exercise, vocal ranges need not be strictly observed and occasional
   overlaps are permissible. The soprano tones given are Handel's.

* = accented PT

2. **Melody**. Use $\frac{6}{3}$ chords wherever appropriate.

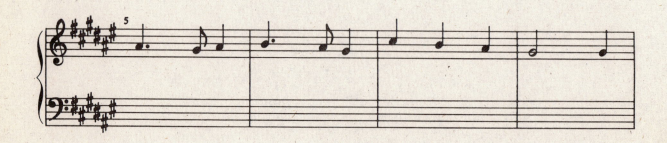

NAME _____

1. Haydn, Piano Sonata No. 48, Hob. XVI/35, III

How does the passage in parallel $^6_3$'s function in a larger context?

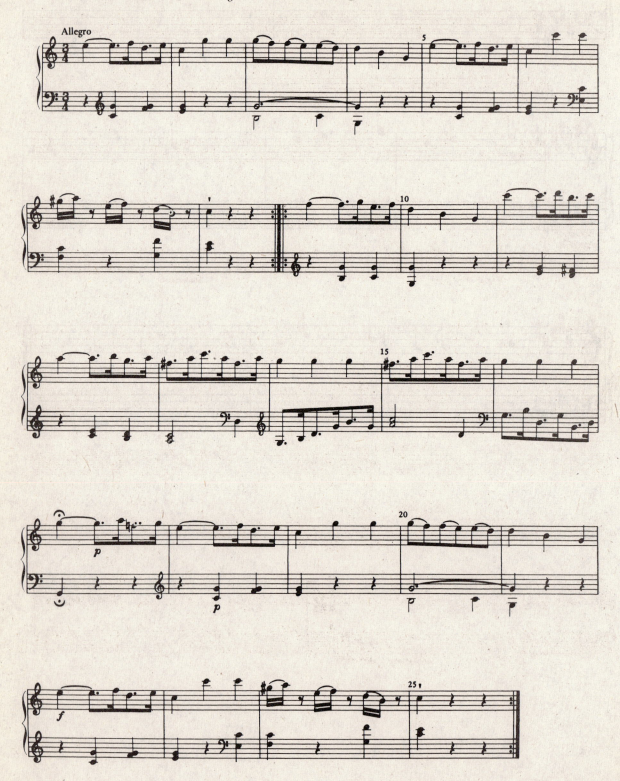

2. Mozart, Trio

(from *Così fan tutte*, K. 588)

How does the passage in parallel $^6_3$'s function in a larger context?

NAME _____

Translation: Again and again we shall drink to the god of love, . . .

3. Mozart, Priests' March (from *The Magic Flute*, K. 620)

How does the passage in parallel $^6_3$'s function in a larger context?

NAME _____

(a)

Translation: What is the hunter looking for here by the millstream? Stay in your own territory, you brazen poacher!

(b)

Translation: Otherwise the doe in the garden will indeed be frightened . . .

5. Schubert, "Du bist die Ruh," D. 776

(Langsam)

Du bist die Ruh, der Frie - de mild, die Sehn - sucht du, und was sie

stillt.

Translation: You are rest and gentle peace, you are yearning and its ful-fillment.

6. Chopin, Nocturne, Op. 48/1

Lento

mezza voce

$\frac{6}{4}$ - Chord Techniques

Preliminaries

Strong and Weak Beats

Put in correct bar lines, using $\frac{2}{4}$ and $\frac{3}{4}$ only. The first and last measures may be incomplete. In some cases two versions are possible.

184 **Melody and Bass-Line Fragments**

Supply figured bass where needed.

Longer Assignments

Melodies and Basses 1

1. **Outer voices, unfigured bass.**

2. **Outer voices, unfigured bass.**

NAME _____

186   3. **Melody.**

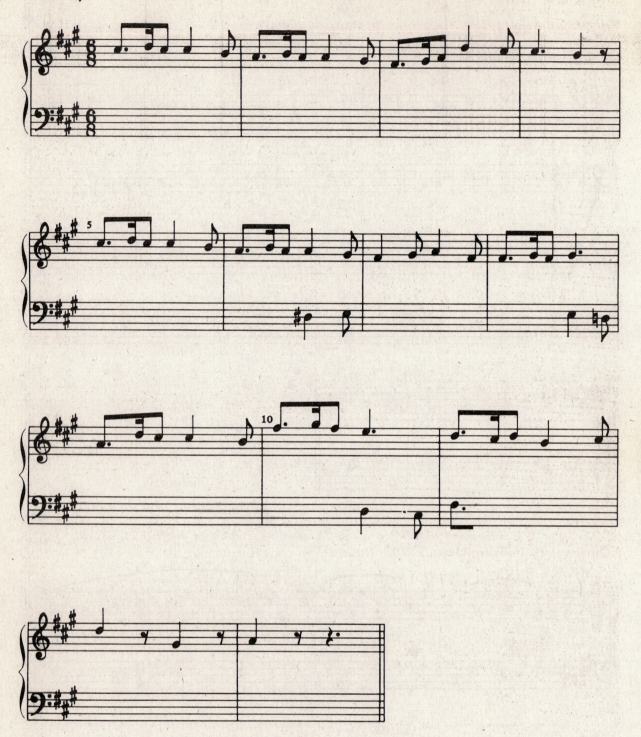

1. Figured bass.

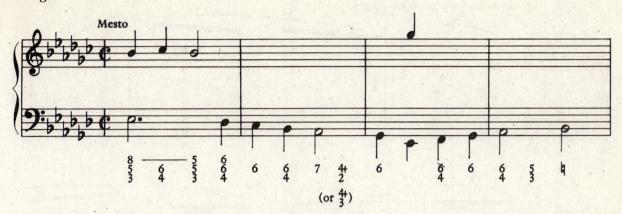

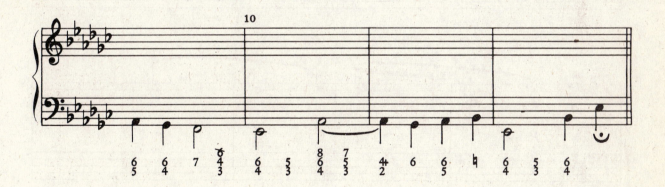

188 2. **Melody.** Use $\frac{6}{4}$ chords at the starred points.

Study and Analysis

Explain the function of each $\frac{6}{4}$ chord.

1. Corelli, Trio Sonata, Op. 1/1, Allegro

2. Bach, "Denn das Gesetz"

(from *Jesu, meine Freude*, BWV 227, IV)

Denn das Ge — setz des Geistes, der da le — ben — dig

Denn, denn das Ge — setz des Gei —

ma — chet in Chri-sto Je — — su, in Chri — sto Je — su,

— stes, der da le — ben — — dig ma — chet in Chri — sto Je — su,

Translation: For the law of the Spirit, which flourishes in Christ Jesus . . .

NAME _____

c:

4. Bach, Cantata 82, I

5. Bach, Aria, "Grosser Herr"   (from *Christmas Oratorio*, BWV 248)

NAME _____

6. Mozart, "O zittre nicht"   (from *The Magic Flute*, K. 620)

What is unusual about the treatment of the starred chord?

Translation: You will go to set her free . . .

7. Mozart, Violin Sonata, K. 296, III

8. Beethoven, Piano Sonata, Op. 2/1, II

9. Beethoven, Symphony No. 6, Op. 68 ("Pastorale"), I

10. Beethoven, Piano Sonata, Op. 78, II

11. Schubert, "Eifersucht und Stolz"   (from *Die schöne Müllerin*, D. 795)   **195**

(Geschwind)

Kehr um, kehr um, und schilt erst dei - ne Mül - le - rin für

ih - ren leich - ten, lo - sen, klei - nen Flat - ter - sinn,

Translation: Come back and chide your milleress for her thoughtless, fickle, petty, and flirtatious ways . . .

12. Schubert, Piano Sonata, D. 850, IV

Allegro moderato

NAME _____

Discuss the unusual treatment of $\frac{6}{4}$.

14. Schumann, "Du Ring an meinem Finger"   (from *Frauenliebe und Leben*, Op. 42)

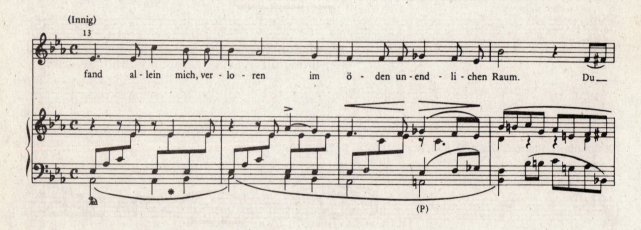

Translation: [I] found myself alone, lost in a bleak and boundless space. Oh ring on my finger . . .

15. Brahms, "O kühler Wald," Op. 72/3

weht, sind ver - weht.

Translation: (The songs) are dispersed.

16. Brahms, Sapphische Ode, Op. 94/4

Ro - sen brach ich nachts mir am dunk - len Ha - ge;

Translation: At night I would pick roses on the dark meadows;

NAME _____

17. Brahms, "Schön war, das ich dir weihte," Op. 95/7

Schön war, das ich dir weih - te, das gol-de - ne Ge-schmei -

de; süss war der Lau - te

Translation: Lovely was the golden jewelry with which I honored you; sweet was the lute's [tone] . . .